RANKIN'S 2020

PHOTOGRAPHS OF A YEAR LIKE NO OTHER

Contents

Chapter 05
Family

Chapter 06
Nature

2020:RANKIN

*This book was made to support the
series "Rankin's 2020" for Sky Arts.
All episodes are available to watch
with Sky TV on demand.*

Foreword

2020 has been a year unlike any other. From powerful protests to the Covid-19 Pandemic, never before have I felt like I am living through such important historical moments. Everyone now has a camera in their pocket and, because of this, I wanted to celebrate the power of photography as a way to help us reflect on these unprecedented times.

So I asked the public to help me create a photo album of this year, to create a record and legacy of what we have all gone through - and they didn't disappoint. Both amateur and professional photographers shared their year with me, in what has turned out to be my biggest project to date. With over 21,000 submissions, people used lockdown and the uncertain nature of this year to pick up their smartphones or their cameras, and to express themselves.

In picking my favourite images to share on Sky Arts, in the show 'Rankin's 2020', and here in this book, I found it difficult at first to define what I was looking for. I was not looking for technical perfection. I was not looking for things I had seen before, or tropes or a particular style. I realised I was looking for an emotional connection. A feeling that bonded me with the images and photographers. An understanding of a shared time, place and feeling.

Across six themes (Empathy, Beauty, Family, Fun, Self, Nature) this project let me explore what 2020 was for us all. Bringing me together with people from around the world, all using photography to capture a moment in time to express how we feel for the future.

Rankin

5

01
Empathy

During 2020 empathy has been a big part of our lives. For me, this category is so important as it includes everything from documentary photography, to shots of carers and NHS workers, to street photography and everyday images that convey deep emotions.

As a photographer, empathy is the most important feeling I can convey. When you create an image with empathy at its heart, not only can you relate to the subject of the photograph, but you can actually feel what the sitter is feeling. I use empathy to relate to the people I photograph, because, I believe, when you can better understand your model as an individual you are better placed to represent who they really are to the viewer.

Rankin

Camera: Leica M10R
ISO: 100
Shutter Speed: 1/500
Aperture: F/2
Lens: 50mm

Rankin

I love documentary photography, some of my biggest inspirations when starting out were documentary photographers, however it is not my bread and butter as a photographer. So for my empathy picture I wanted to put my portraiture spin on a documentary subject.

I chose to photograph Arlene Wellman, Chief Nurse at Epsom and St Helier University Hospitals NHS Trust, because for me she stands for all of the overwhelming empathy that has been exhibited during 2020 and the Covid Pandemic. From Clap for Carers to volunteering at local charities, people have been showing their support and care for others like never before. As a nurse, Arlene epitomises this as she deals in empathy every day.

The portrait photographer in me really chose to focus on Arlene's eyes. With her looking out at the camera there is an instant connection between her and the viewer. The authenticity of this connection being mirrored in my choice to shoot the image in colour. There can be a tendency for photographers to shoot documentary subjects in black and white, believing it connotes a sense of historical seriousness, but, for me, the primary colours in this image really speak to the emergency nature of what is happening around us and that brings the image to life.

Tips

01   Rankin used a 50mm lens for his Empathy portrait, but a wide angle 28mm or 35mm lens works better for documentary photography.

02   Don't default to black and white for documentary photographs, colour can be equally impactful.

03   When shooting documentary photography, a small quiet camera can help you be unobtrusive and discreet.

Yrsa Daley-Ward

I was walking through Fort Green Park every morning in lockdown to try and keep my spirits up. The plaque was on a bench and it spoke to me, so I took a picture for myself. It made me think about my own mother, about life, and how we miss people, especially during lockdown.

Felix Russell-Saw

This image was taken at the Bristol Black Lives Matter protest, where the Edward Colston statue had just been toppled. My friend Mano got on the plinth and shared his thoughts on being a young black man in the city, while I shot a roll of film faster than I ever have in my life. I sold prints of the picture raising just over £10,000 for SARI (Stand Against Racism and Inequality) and I am grateful the image has given back to the community.

Location: Bristol
Level: Professional

"There is something symbolic about this picture, something dignified and elegant. I love the way the photographer has composed it, especially the way that all of the placards at the bottom are surrounding the plinth. They draw you in and take you up into the image.

Rankin

Nigel Humphriss

Sadly, my mum had a stroke at the start of the year. When she was struggling in the hospital I raced down to see her and, when I got there, I found my dad lost in his thoughts staring at Mum. After 60 years of marriage, this is the love you find.

Location: London
Level: Non-Professional

"I love how intimate we're able to be, how close we're able to get. We're not bystanders looking on, we're directly in this, we see the emotion that's happening between them. I love that it's all about love, I love the story that it tells me, it's worth a million novels.

16

Yrsa Daley-Ward

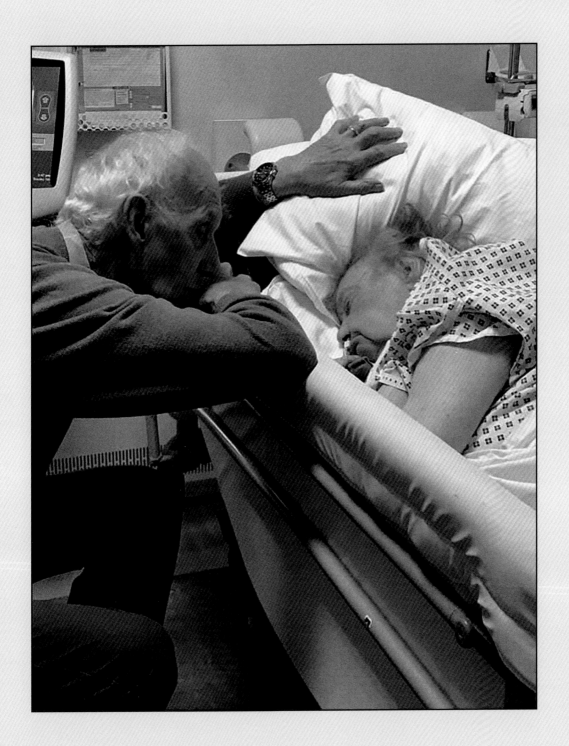

Rod Olukoya

In the middle of all the uniforms, there was a lady in a white t-shirt. I was struck by the way she moved so serenely, yet there was all this madness going on around her. That captured the moment, the feeling of the day - people had just had enough.

Location: London
Level: Semi-Professional

"I thought the subject matter was fascinating, it was interesting to see how Rod approached this image. You do get that uncertain feeling of "what happened next?"

Caroline Hunter

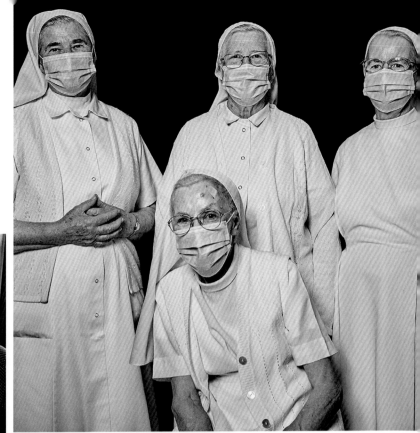

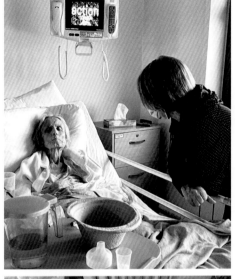

23

Steve Tanner

Cutting my eight-year-old son's hair in the bath. I felt a moment of déjà vu; the sound of scissors, falling hair, smell of shampoo and the itching of hair on skin and lightness of the head. Visceral memories of childhood.

Location: Cornwall
Level: Professional

"What I like about this image is that it leaves lots of questions unanswered. I like the soft clumps of hair mixed with the wisps of hair. I wasn't sure whether, initially, it suggested empathy but there was an intimacy about it that kept me interested.

Caroline Hunter

25

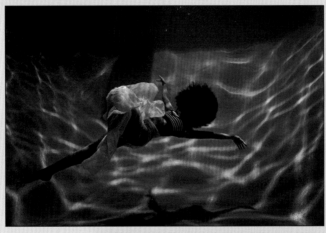

02
Beauty

Beauty means so many different things to so many different people, which is what excites me about it as a category. It can be glamorous and about perfection, but I also love using beauty photography to explore ideas and experimenting with concepts.

Over the last few years I have seen beauty photography become a powerful mode of expression. I think today's beauty photography – one that explores the ways we use cosmetics, or choose not to use cosmetics, to express ourselves – is a really exciting thing. It's about being able to construct a new way of looking at yourself or others, and showing that to the world.

Rankin

Camera: Hasselblad H6X
ISO: 100
Shutter Speed: 1/320
Aperture: F/16
Lens: 80mm

2020:BEAUTY

Rankin

During lockdown I did a portrait series for the NHS where I developed a new way of shooting from behind a plastic screen. The necessity of this separation between myself and who I was photographing was perhaps the hardest thing emotionally I had to come up against at work during lockdown. I love to talk with and really get to know who I photograph, and suddenly I couldn't even shake their hand. This is why, for my beauty image, I chose to use the plastic sheeting and tear it open, to release myself from lockdown visually.

Shot just as we got to go back into work, I really felt Grace, and their self expression through drag, was the perfect metaphor for that feeling of being set free through beauty. Shooting with a sharp focus but with soft lighting I wanted to allow Grace the space to really explore their beauty whilst celebrating the release from confinement that the end of summer 2020 allowed me.

Tips

01   An 80mm lens on a medium format camera provides a perspective view that is true to the human eye.

02   Rankin likes to shoot at a 320 shutter speed. Shooting at a high shutter speed, when using flash, eliminates any ambient light that may affect your image.

03   When shooting on a smartphone, control the exposure setting to create professional looking images.

Val Garland

I was in lockdown with my godchild, she said, "Auntie Val, you've got your make-up here, let's have a play" and we started playing. Instead of just doing a lip shot, I went in and thought, "that's far more interesting". I painted more pink on, so it felt like the lip was bleeding and that just felt more interesting to me.

Andrew Quinn

Recently, men have become open to exhibiting more feminine qualities such as empathy and sensitivity. Society's views on gender are slowly changing as a greater number of people are realising that they can express themselves in a more fluid way. I want my viewer to look at this image and feel like it is now celebrated for men to express themselves in a more modern way, liberated from traditional gender stereotypes.

Location: London
Level: Photography Graduate

"I felt like it was a very natural way of interpreting beauty. What I really like about Andrew's image is that it has quite a sculptural quality to it. I like the fact that it's a profile but you see both of his eyes.

What I think is interesting about this image is that you see the changes of texture. The texture of his dreadlocks through to the pores of his skin, then you see the smoothness of the shirt.

Caroline Hunter

33

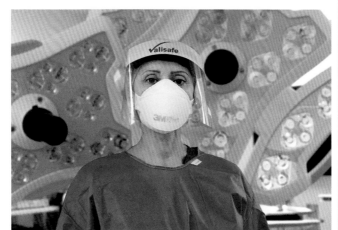

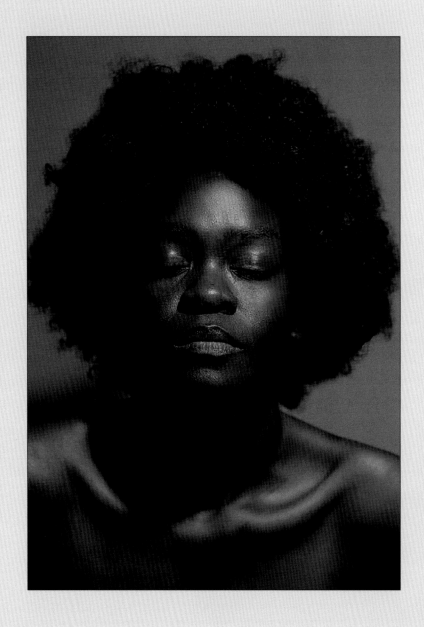

Location: Thornton Heath
Level: Non-Professional

Chris Bovell

Beauty tends to be viewed by how refined someone looks, how perfect someone appears - I wanted to do something that celebrated truth, rawness and reality. I deliberately chose to do this shoot in black and white because it strips everything down to its rawness, it makes it more gritty, it makes it more real. Patience really comes out as natural and beautiful. She's so confident and comfortable in her skin.

"I love raw beauty. I think this whole idea of absolutely everything being Facetuned and perfect is not so real. With this image I love the fact that Patience was just beautiful in her own skin.

Val Garland

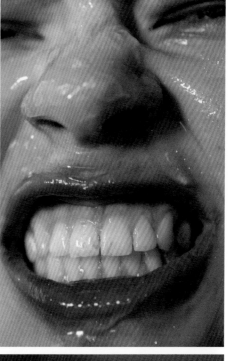

Mark Kelly

When I was doing street photography, I got talking to Kenya and they told me how they use make-up in order to express how they are feeling on a day-to-day basis. 2020 has shown us that we should not take someone's state of mind for granted. Not everyone can display their feelings on the outside as Kenya does.

Location: Surrey
Level: Professional

"It's one of those pictures where you go, "what is this picture about?" I couldn't work it out.

I think when a photograph intrigues you that much, it's definitely doing something right.

Rankin

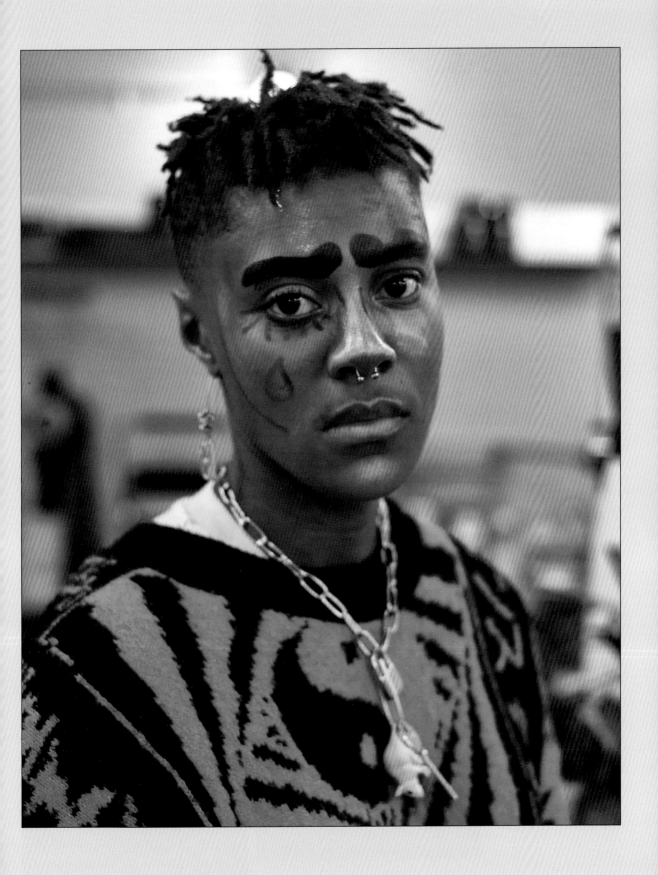

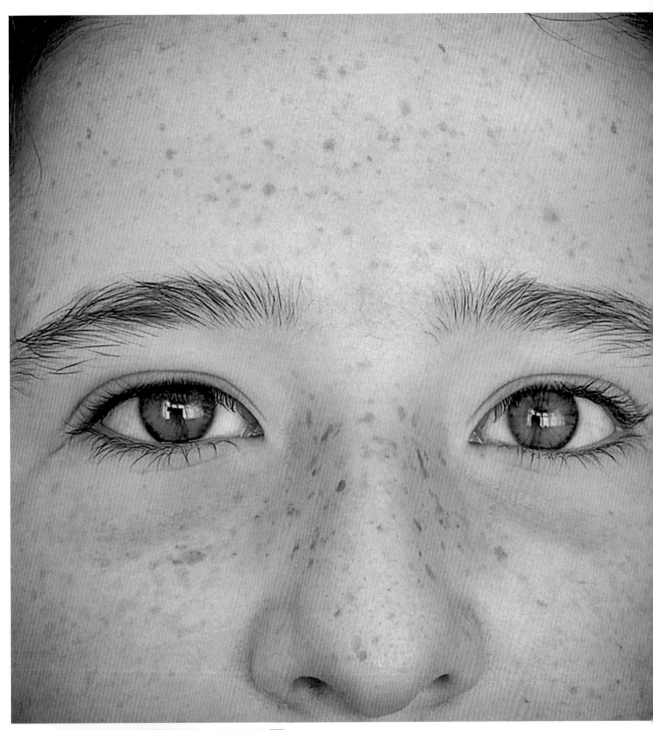

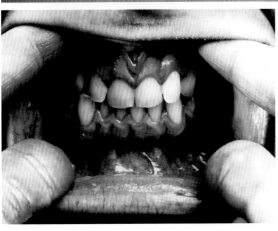

Tina Eisen

This picture sums up 2020 for me as it embodies the very moment lockdown hit every photographer. In order to keep creating, we had to become a four man team in one. We could no longer be with models, or photographic assistants, so we had to become them.

As a beauty photographer I had no way of creating and expressing myself so this image was born out of desperation, doing the makeup on my own lips, photographing and retouching it.

Location: Milton Keynes
Level: Professional

"I don't like perfection, I like imperfection, and this is perfect in its imperfection. I think that's what makes it work.

I also love the lipstick on the teeth. It's sexy.

Val Garland

45

03
Self

For the longest time I have been obsessed with the self-portrait, or rather the "selfie" as it's now more commonly known. A great selfie is an expression of who you are and where you see yourself fitting into the world around you. A way of really exploring yourself as an individual.

It can be the most incredibly difficult and yet creatively stimulating challenge. A true self-portrait is not taken at arm's length, just for the social media likes, it is instead a real moment for introspection.

They can be serious, funny, or political statements - but ultimately a great self-portrait should truly be you.

Rankin

Rankin

Selfies are everywhere. They are the most ubiquitous image online, as social media has made everyone into their own personal brand. Every day, by the millions, people are creating a two-dimensional version of themselves at the perfect angle, with the most flattering light, and with any apparent flaws removed. The images all look the same and don't say anything!

For my self-portrait image I wanted to make a statement. I chose to write "SELL FIE" to really underline the fact that, for me, I see selfies as just a way of selling yourself or your lifestyle. They are all surface.

To take a true self-portrait, I tell people to think about the image they're making, not just what they look like. Treat your smartphone like a camera, rather than a mirror.

Tips

01
For best results don't mix natural and artificial light.

02
Use the back-facing camera to take your selfies. Not only does the back-facing camera have a better lens and sensor, but you'll get a better image if you're not looking at yourself on the screen.

03
It's worth investing in a tripod and using your phone's timer to take your self-portraits.

Kelly Knox

For me, it's about that raw, authentic, unique beauty.
No masks, no filter, this is who I am. This is me.

"When I saw the image I thought of Greek scultpure, for some reason, I think it's the pose. There's a pose called contrapposto where you subtly shift your body and it creates a dynamism. Kelly here has become a sort of Athena character.

Aindrea Emelife

51

Aurora Way

Lockdown changed my life as an artist, I spent most of my days taking hundreds of photos and arranging flowers for more inspiration. By the end I brought it all together in this image; the photos I created, the concept sketches and research scribbles.

I loved the forced growth of lockdown, I will seek isolation like this for the rest of my life. I will remember the gift of creating every day, of being lost in those moments.

Location: Hampshire
Level: Professional

"I feel like she was going into bloom, with a different and awakened sense of self.

Kelly Knox

"Here digital editing software is used for the right reasons. She isn't using technology to change or retouch herself, she is using it as a mode of expression.

Rankin

Location: Angoulême, France
Level: Self-Taught

This picture of me holding my reflection in my hand reminds me of how strong I can be despite the situation.

Originally I took this picture in 2013 when I was feeling lost, anxious and trapped. During the lockdown in France, I found a version of this self-portrait in my digital archives. I decided to take a picture of it from my computer screen, using a film camera, because I was experiencing a similar feeling and I wanted to make it timeless.

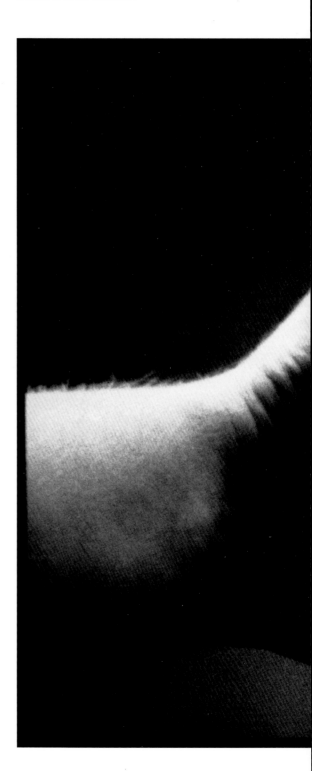

"I was drawn to this image because it was so ambiguous. I like that the image was re-shot through a digital screen as it makes me think of 2020 and how we've had to live through screens.

Caroline Hunter

Clothilde
Bertin Lalande

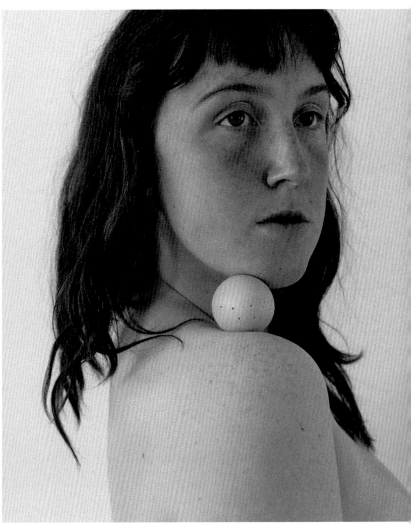

Esther Poyer

One of my lockdown activities has been "at home spa moments". I took the photo with the front camera on my iPhone XS from the light of the living room window, while I air-dried as per the instructions for the herbal bath I'd just had. I called the photograph "Ascension" because this to me is a sign of our times, this journey from birth to death and rebirth - it feels like the entire planet is being reborn right now.

Location: Greater London
Level: Non-Professional

"Technically, I think it's a well-conceived picture and I want to know more about her. I love how the background goes from dark to light, and her face goes from light to dark. She feels very content and accepting of the world.

Rankin

Kim Wong

I wanted to capture my overwhelming anxiety and frustration during the first few weeks of lockdown. My intention wasn't to shoot a self-portrait, but to concentrate on the monotony of constantly being instructed to wash our hands. In doing so, hoping to safeguard myself and my family from the awful pandemic outside.

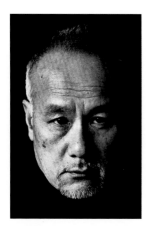

Location: East Sussex
Level: Non-Professional

"What drew me to this image is I feel there's a great sense of mystery behind it. It's very raw, I could sense a sadness, a depression, or a low emotional feeling and I wanted to know if he was OK. This speaks very much of 2020 lockdown to me, and all the emotions people have felt in this period.

Kelly Knox

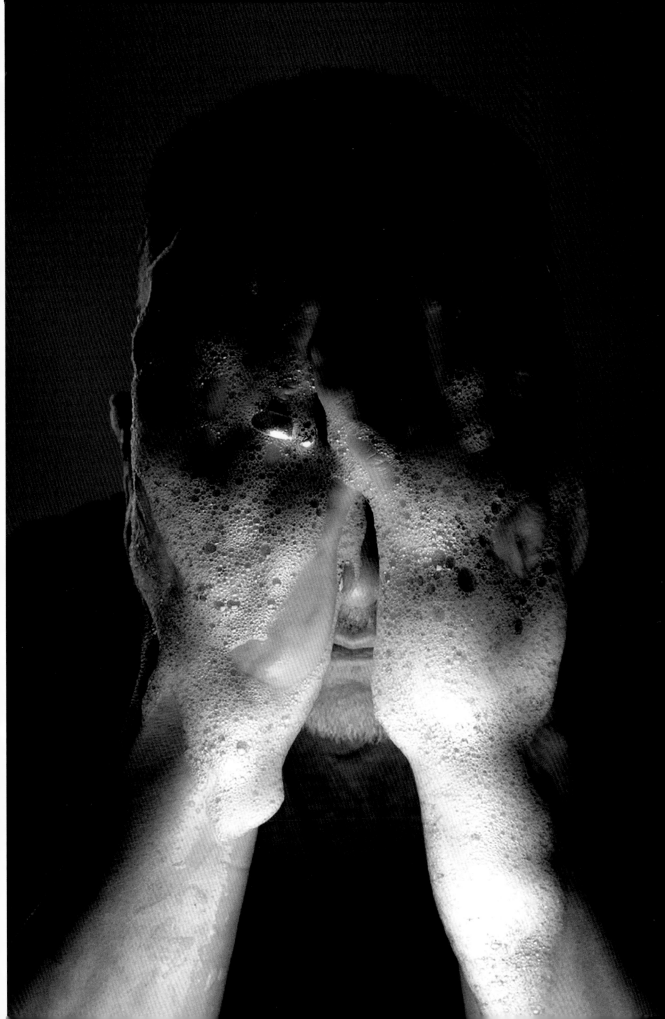

Erin G. Wesley

My quarantine life in a photo. A cinematographer turned banana bread baking, cooking and cleaning, satin PJ wearing queen.

Location: Los Angeles
Level: Director of Photography

"What I love about this image is that I could see myself in it. This is that in-between which we all experienced in lockdown: getting dressed up for a meeting at 11am and then doing the washing up at half past.

Aindrea Emelife

04
Fun

At first glance, 2020 could seem like the year that cancelled fun. Whether you were set to enjoy a sporting event, go on holiday or party at a music festival - 2020 had other plans. But that doesn't mean we were unable to find new ways to enjoy ourselves. Millions of us took up new hobbies and creativity was back in the home.

Whether you were taking up yoga, painting with your kids, or putting on a socially distanced street party; this category captured those moments that kept us feeling positive, connected with our communities and sharing a laugh with friends. Proving there was plenty of fun this year to celebrate.

Rankin

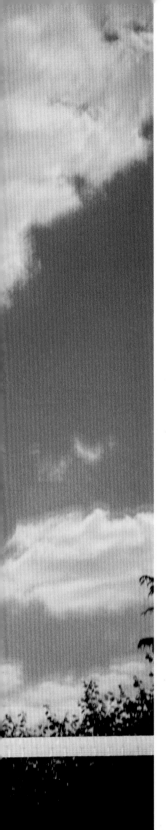

Camera: Mamiya RZ67
Shutter Speed: 1/400
Aperture: F/32
Lens: 65mm
Film Stock: Kodak Portra 400

Rankin

Jaquelyn Ogunwale, a world ranking junior tennis player, was the perfect choice for how I felt about fun in 2020. When lockdown restrictions were eased, she was finally able to get back out onto the court and do what she enjoys most. You could see how excited she was to return to her passion and I wanted to capture that exuberance in a way that represented my enjoyment at getting back to photographing people.

I decided to use my workhorse camera, the camera I used for most of the first twenty years of my career. Using a fill in flash to really make her pop against the bright summer day, this image really demonstrates how I used to shoot for most of the nineties and early noughties. This method of shooting takes me back to a way of working which really cemented my passion for photography.

Collaborating with Jaquelyn to find an action shot, one which really showcased her skill and drive to succeed at her sport, brought the fun back to my work - something which I felt 2020 had been lacking for months.

Tips

01

Shooting at a higher shutter speed reduces motion blur and freezes the action in your images.

02

By using a fill in flash you can brighten deep shadows, it's particularly useful when shooting outdoors on sunny days - especially when the background is brighter than the subject you're photographing.

03

Don't be afraid to try photographing from different angles, Rankin likes to shoot from below as it gives the person being photographed a strong and iconic look.

Layton Williams

My friend had a place in Spain so I said, "let's just go for a couple of weeks". I probably wasn't smiling the next day after this picture, as I think that's when we found out we'd have to go into quarantine. It encapsulates my happy times.

"This image captures everything we all missed during 2020 lockdown.

Brett Rogers

Adam Batterbee

It was my first visit to see a friend, who is an avid collector of weird stuff, after lockdown. She'd given her "doll squad" the full COVID safety treatment. The squad looked fantastic and was already set up sitting in a drawer - I took the shot.

Location: Hertfordshire
Level: Professional

"This really exemplifies 2020 and all the constraints we've all had to suffer, including the fact we're having to wear masks every day. Here humour is introduced because the masks are made out of dishcloths. Humour is everywhere but there's a serious and rather dark underside.

Brett Rogers

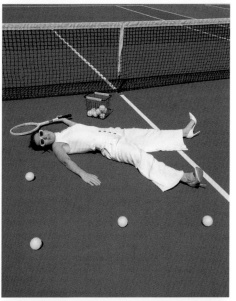

Loukia Yiolides

Seeing Gabrielle every day during lockdown brought me joy and happiness. We would meet outside the front of our houses to play, exercise, tell stories, and try to keep things as normal as possible. We would make everything fun, so hula-hooping was easy for her, two was a challenge but Gaby knew I was going to take a photograph so the challenge was on.

Location: Croydon
Level: Non-Professional

"This picture is unadulterated fun, it's brilliant. What I love about it is the eye contact tells you she is having such a good laugh. She's really looking at the camera, there's no holds barred.

Rankin

Megan Ashburner

I took my little boy to a lake near where we live to explore. It was the wettest day, but he had the best time jumping off rocks into puddles. I only had my mobile phone, but managed to capture this magical moment.

Location: Lake District
Level: Non-Professional

"I just like how free that little boy is. Even though it's a cloudy day, he's making the most of it in his wellies. That's 2020, we're going to get out in the clouds and the rain and we're still going to have fun, because what else can we do?

Layton Williams

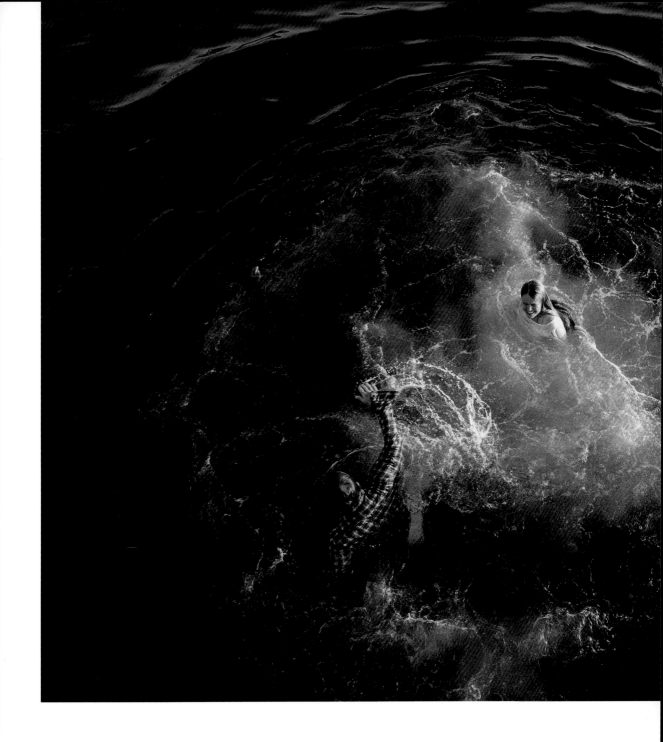

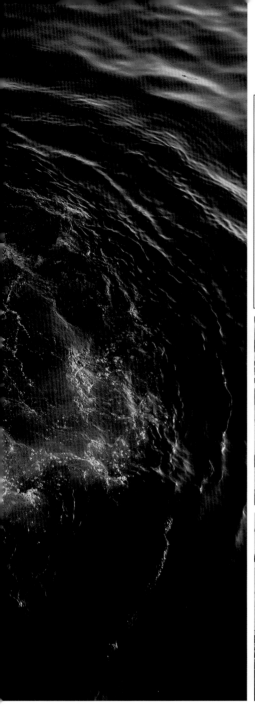

Tracy Vine

During lockdown I completely self-isolated for four months and being confined to the house and small garden for that amount of time had its challenges. Photography was my way of dealing with how I was feeling. I was missing going to art galleries, so I created my own art gallery scene using miniatures.

Location: Essex
Level: Semi-Professional

"This is what we need to cheer ourselves up. Such invention and creativity! I'm trying to work out which modern artist she's sending up, could it be Damien Hirst and his works using medicine tablets?

Brett Rogers

"What I loved about her image is that she's created this little world when she can't get out into the real world. It's an amazing premise, it's so smart.

Rankin

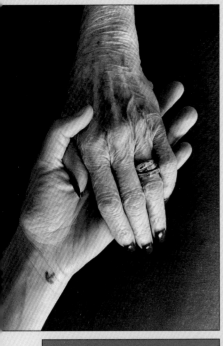

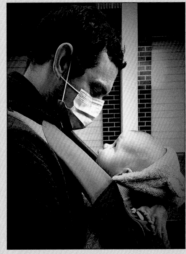

05
Family

The category Family is one we can all relate to, as it has been such a strong focus for many of us in lockdown this year. Whether your family is by birth, or you think of your friends as your family, it is a defining feature of all our lives and is really meaningful for us to record.

Personally, my favourite photographs will always be those I've taken of my loved ones. I have had the honour of seeing people around me grown and change, and I have been able to capture this all through my photography. I think the best portraits come out of the photographer having a strong connection with their sitter, and who better to connect with than your family.

Rankin

Rankin

I chose to photograph my nephew Riley using one of my oldest cameras. It's a camera that has a special place in my heart because it is one of the first I can ever remember seeing. I always think there is something almost romantic for me about shooting on film, it is how I began my career and there is this sense of permanence in taking an image and it existing physically forever. As a medium it carries such sentimental value, which makes it the perfect choice to capture images of people I love.

I find a real authenticity to images shot on film. Unlike digital photos people cannot demand to see the results straight away and they cannot delete the images just because their hair isn't perfect. There is a great deal of anticipation when you're waiting for your film to develop and getting to relive and share back moments at a later date is incredible. I'm always more inclined to look back through printed photographs over digital files on my phone or computer.

Tips

01 Don't be put off by overcast days. Flat lighting can help hide imperfections in the skin by giving you a soft and even light, making it great for portrait photography.

02 Rankin used Kodak Portra 400 medium format film. It is known for its warmth and strength of colour, making it great for skin tones.

03 If you are shooting on film, you can use your smartphone to check the lighting and composition of your images before using your camera.

Jamal Edwards

This was before lockdown, I was shooting an advert and I wanted to include my mum in it. 2020 was the year my mum got a new job after she had a bit of a down moment and this was an up moment for us. That was what made it 2020 for me, because it was a new decade, and we could look forward to the next ten years.

"She looks like she's emerging with such confidence

Brett Rogers

95

Chris Harrison

I'm not sure how much of this year Eva will really remember. But that weekly event of going out at eight o'clock on a Thursday to Clap for Carers - shouting, screaming, singing and banging a pan - I think that'll be one of her key memories. Thankfully I've got a photograph of her doing it too.

Location: London
Level: Non-Professional

"This image could have easily been cliché but because it really captures a moment, it becomes such a fantastic picture.

Rankin

Hannah Mordi

My sons, Memphis (3) and Nelson (1) had been playing outside in the paddling pool and had come in to dry off. I found them on the sofa looking at Nelson's favourite book together. Memphis had his favourite foam sword in hand and it looked to me like he was protecting his younger brother. The light was beautiful, so I took their picture.

Location: London
Level: Non-Professional

"If you have kids you'll recognise them in this picture. Their relationship is so evident and so true.

Rankin

"I like it because it's quite raw, she hasn't said "pose for the picture". She's just taken it candidly.

Jamal Edwards

Julie Bannon

Sneaking a photo of my son in our steamed up car, whilst waiting on our fish and chips after our daily lockdown walk. I have studied every part of his face during lockdown, it is now imprinted in my heart.

Location: Dundee
Level: Non-Professional

"There's a very long tradition of great photographers like Philip-Lorca diCorcia who use light in this particular way to frame a face, it looks like a cinematic still.

Brett Rogers

"This image is so strong because of the light in it. You've got this device which is totally absorbing Julie's son and highlighting his concentration due to its bright screen. This artificial light really stands out against the blue, cold, still light from outside the car door.

Rankin

Seona Misumi

At the start of lockdown, until we found our feet with it, we found every day feeling like a Sunday but with none of the swimming or gymnastics classes and week ahead prep we usually do. But we knew it was essential to keep us all safe. In a busy world, where time is our most precious commodity, it's been eye-opening to realise how busy we are. I don't think we will go back to the levels of busy that we were before.

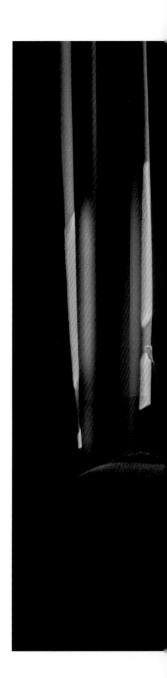

Location: Glasgow
Level: Professional

"I think it perfectly captures the whole feeling we had in lockdown of being behind the walls of the family home. Looking out to the beautiful sunshine, I'm sure these children are wishing they could be out and about playing, and yet both of them are totally absorbed in their own imagination, their own worlds.

Brett Rogers

06
Nature

Nature is a fascinating category because it spans everything from epic landscapes to intimate wildlife portraits. Whilst we were all in lockdown, the natural world flourished. Minimal air pollution, minimal disruption to wildlife and the natural world, all meant photographers where able to capture scenes in unprecedented surroundings.

But nature photography isn't all documentary out in the wilderness. The natural world has permeated all of our surroundings. Whether it is a sunset over a city, flowers delivered to a loved one, or household pets, photographing and appreciating nature can take place anywhere. Making this one of the most versatile categories to photograph.

Rankin

Camera: Canon EOS 1D
ISO: 400
Shutter Speed: 1/125
Aperture: F/8
Lens: 24 - 105mm

Rankin

When we first went into lockdown, I found myself feeing really angry and frustrated. I'm a workaholic and for the first time in my career I couldn't go to the studio and create work with my team. Instead I created a makeshift studio for still life work in my home and, in the place of photographing portraits of models and celebrities, I started trying to take portraits of flowers.

The first time I set a flower on fire it was incredible therapy for me. It took me quite a while to actually set fire to them, because I was almost too in awe of their beauty, but in destruction you got a real sense of jeopardy, change and transformation. It was all of life right there in one moment.

Through the process of creation I was finding a way to embrace working alone, alongside using natural imagery as a cypher for the wider world. Nature on fire, perhaps the perfect metaphor for 2020.

Tips

01   When shooting still life, use a clean and simple backdrop so the background doesn't interfere with the image you're creating.

02   Rankin prefers to shoot nature using natural light as it makes the images feel more authentic.

03   To help capture flames that appear sharper and in focus, Rankin uses a 125 shutter speed and a DSLR camera that can capture up to 10 frames per second.

Jaime Winstone

When lockdown happened we got out of London, it felt like the end of the world, Mother Nature coming crashing down. On this day the sun was shining and the tree was glowing, it had come to life, it had blossomed overnight. It was so majestic, it was like "this is my moment" and it was a symbol of hope for me.

"This tree was beautiful, the whole shape of it, the light on it. It feels like it's saying "Take a look at me, I am so beautiful and I want to see some respect and appreciation."

Carol Allen-Storey

Anil Mistry

Whilst having an evening sea swim during the heatwave, I took my waterproof camera in with me to capture the sunset. I accidentally fired off my camera whilst kicking out with my feet to stay afloat, and the resulting image captured the splash along with the sun distorted through drops of water on the lens, which created a magnificent liquid fiery blur in the centre of frame.

Location: Shoreham-by-Sea
Level: Professional

"The colours look dreamlike.
The amber reminds me of
a Turner painting.

Aindrea Emelife

"It is exactly how I felt, and I'm
pretty sure most people felt,
as lockdown was happening
- it was like a wave coming at
us. What is different though,
for me, is the sunset because
that's the optimism for the
future behind it.

Rankin

Fiona MacLeod Cameron

I call this image "Out of Office". Nature is the new office.

Location: Inverness
Level: Non-Professional

"It's nature but there's an office chair that's found itself in this unlikely position. It's got nostalgic elements. It's also got humour, with the dots on the quilted back which make it look like it's smiling or having a cheeky grin. It looks at the idea of working from home in the most obvious sense and how offices and our working habits have changed.

Aindrea Emelife

121

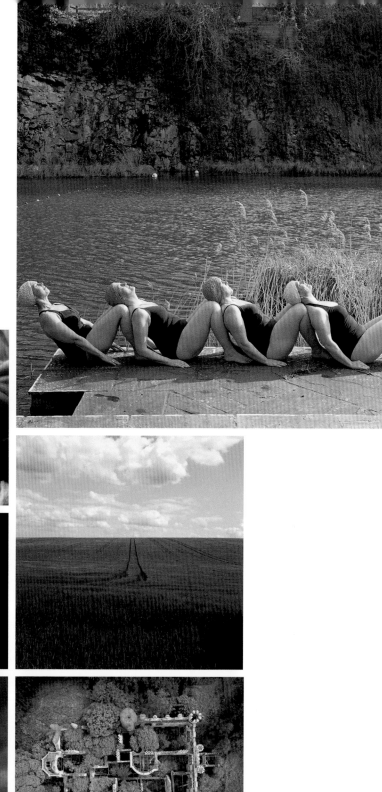

George Vasilopoulos

This is Winstanley Estate from my rooftop as storm clouds rolled in. it was just before sunset, yet the thick black clouds made for an eerie ambience, almost like moonlight, with a Tim Burton-esque feel.

Location: London
Level: Professional

"Nature is in the foreground. Nature is taking the first steps of saying, "I'm recovering my land from the footprint of man". For me, nature is visually the more dominant force than the urban life of the rest of the picture.

Carol Allen-Storey

Logan Steppert

A long-planned trip with Ross Halfin to Death Valley. Got to Zabriskie Point by sunrise, and salt flats by breakfast. Back to West Hollywood just before 4pm.

Location: Los Angeles
Level: Non-Professional

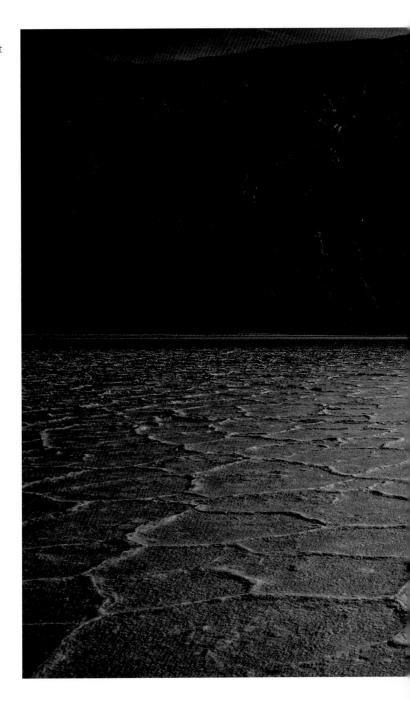

"I love this picture because of the vastness of it and the textures of land it covers. It makes me think about how insignificant we are as humans on this earth. It's such a powerful image because it puts nature and the world into perspective.

Jaime Winstone

Marcia Harding

Walking through the cemetery taking in the stillness made me feel positive and at ease. The carpet of bluebells spreading around the gravestones felt like nature was reclaiming the space. The burst of vivid colour and beautiful scent heightened my senses - I lay down amongst the bluebells and took the photograph, capturing the moment.

Location: Manchester
Level: Non-Professional

"A good photo should speak to your emotions. So to be able to take a picture like this, which will always draw an emotion from you, is a triumph for a photographer.

Aindrea Emelife

"I think it's a very beautiful piece and really important to have something that helps you to take back ownership of what it is to lose someone.

Jaime Winstone

Credits

All credits listed in the order images appear,
from left to right, on the page.

Chapter 01
Empathy

Chapter 02
Beauty

Chapter 03
Self

Chapter 04
Fun

Chapter 05
Family

Chapter 06
Nature

Mental Health UK

This book has been made in support of Mental Health UK. Profits from the book sales will be going to support this incredible cause.

Mental Health UK connects with people and organisations to provide mental health information, advice and support. They improve understanding and provide vital care – allowing more people across the UK to access support for their own mental health as well as friends, family members and carers.

One in four of us experience mental health problems and living with a mental health condition can affect many aspects of daily life, from your physical health to your home, your work and ability to manage money. Every year the charity provides thousands of people across the UK with practical advice and information to help understand and manage their mental health.

Covid-19 has had a significant impact on people's mental health and Mental Health UK has been working hard to respond to the increased demand for services and support.

Find out more at mentalhealth-uk.org

Mental Health UK is a registered charity. Charity number: 1170815

Copyright

*With thanks to everyone who entered their images. It's been
an incredible honour to see all of your creativity and I hope
your passion for photography will continue for years to come!
Rankin x*

Publisher - Rankin Publishing Ltd.
Editor - Ellen Stone
Design - Alice Daisy Pomfret
Post Production - True Black Studio
Printer - Park Communications

NPL Media Production Team:
Sam Dooey-Miles
Margaret Giles
Nat Low

Sky Arts:
Vanessa Woodard
Benedetta Pinelli
Sam Shields

Made in collaboration with:

 RANKIN Public Offerings Ltd.

ISBN: 978-0-9955741-6-8
© Rankin Publishing, 2020